Musings of a Healing Mind

Jenna Korpas

BookLeaf Publishing

Presentation by *BookLeaf Publishing*

Web: www.bookleafpub.com

E-mail: info@bookleafpub.com

ISBN: 9789395621106

First edition 2022

DEDICATION

This book is dedicated to my daughter, Liv

Thank you for being my best friend, my greatest work of art, and for saving my life

I love you

The Narcissist

Feed the beast
In my ravenous soul
He dwells there deep
And gorges on gold
He steals what's good
And devours it slow
Savoring the pain
While destroying your glow

Carousel

I can still remember the first time I rode the
carousel
The carnival had just come into town
Through the trees I could see it's lustrous body
It was shiny and new and captivating
I was instantly drawn in by the bright flashing
lights
The beautiful vibrant colors and alluring music
The air was full of laughter and excitement
I picked a gilded white horse and I jumped on
Spinning 'round and 'round, it was so much fun
Watching everyone's smiling faces as I rose
Up and down and up and down and
down
down
down
Now 'round and 'round I go atop a rusted horse
The paints chipping away and the lights have all
burnt out
And it doesn't go up anymore, but I can't get off
the ride, not yet
After all I can still enjoy the view
I can still have fun watching everyone smiling in
the crowd but,
Where did everybody go?

The carnival came and went, yet here I am
Still spinning in circle after endless circle
But I have a feeling that next time it'll be
different
I know someone will come to fix the ride
They have to make it move back up again
It's the best part, and the lights, oh the lights
Just let me enjoy the ride one last time
Please just let me have fun again like that first
time
Then I'll get off, I promise I will
Can someone just come fix the fucking lights!
I know you can hear me, why won't you just
help me
Fuck you then!!
I don't want your help anyway!
It's fine like this, I like it better this way you
fucking piece of shit!
And I'm glad everyone's gone
I didn't even like them or their stupid fake grins
anyway
No one's really that happy
Wait no please don't leave me here like this
No, no, fuck I'm sorry I didn't mean it
Please come back and help me!
Just help me,
Somebody
Please

The Devil

Your light shines black
Your fire burns cold
Your twisted demeanor
Can turn diamonds to coal
Your rivers ran dry
Your forests are dead
Your nature of destruction
Is the image of dread

Another Broken Heart

Now my bed feels as empty as the promises you
made
And your clouds hid the sun to turn my skies
grey
These sheets are so lonely in which you once
lain
But what's another broken heart on the way to
the grave

My House Is Haunted By You

Memories playing through every doorway
Like a portal to the past
Your face engrained in my minds eye
How long will it last
Is your ghost with me forever
Like you claimed your love would be
How long until your every touch
Fades from memory
I close my eyes to hear your laugh
See your smile and your gaze
If I reach my hand out far enough
Could I touch you if I prayed
My house is haunted by you
My body is as well
But your spirit keeps me company
In this cold and lonely hell

Lunar Ties

No matter the distance between us
I find comfort in knowing we're looking at the
same moon
That it's glare is shining on you too
Lighting your nights as brightly as you lit mine
And when it sets
Your view will be as dark and cold as how you
left me

Desolate

Abandoned buildings
Filled with stories
Leading to their demise
Decrepit beauty
Still standing through the pain
Empty rooms once occupied
Full of life and warmth
Now all that remains
Is an empty frame

Dying Embers

Your love
Is like a cigarette
I can't put out
So I watch it burn
The toxins I consume
To fill the void
Your absence has left
And when the embers die
I wonder
Will yours soon too

Farewell

I hope that you're happy
But I hope that you cry
I hope you find peace
Through the tears in your eyes
I hope you feel empty
But I hope you're content
I hope you reminisce
On the time we have spent
I hope you feel lonely
But I hope you get by
I hope you're okay
Knowing this is goodbye

tired

I'm tired of trying
Tired of living
I'm tired of lying
Everytime you ask if I'm okay
And I say I'm fine
I'm just a little,
tired

Scars In My Eyes

Just when I think it's getting better
The flashbacks flood my sorrowed mind
Paralyzing me in my own memories
As if time stops
And the world in front of me fades to black
A second can feel like years passing before your
eyes
While reliving the moments you can't lose to
time

Refreshment

Your touch is like a tall glass of water
On a hot summer's day
The wind blowing through the trees
Sounds of distant birds chirping
All is still yet full of life
I close my eyes and suddenly
Everything feels okay

Inner Light

The phases of the moon
Have nothing on you, dear
You turn darkness into light
By transmuting your fears
The moon only reflects
Illumination from the sun
But you glow from within
And that can't be undone

Solarium

Golden sunlight
Falls upon on my face
Caressing my cheek
With it's warm embrace
I am the destination
It's final resting place
Absorb the cosmic rays
Full of divinity and grace

The Language of Time

The universe always finds a way to speak
Communicating in ways the blind can't see
Written in the stars are the transcripts of time
All there has ever been and ever will be
Spread across the endless chasm
Lost upon those who lack transcending eyes

The Observer

You are not your body
You are not your bones
You are not the vessel
Your spirit calls home

You are not your thoughts
You are not your mind
You are not the ego
Your soul hides behind

You are not your worries
You are not your regrets
You are not the memories
Your brain can't forget

You are the observer
You are outside of time
You are conscious awareness
You're infinite and divine

Masterpiece

Your soul is a work of art
That belongs in the Louvre
To be adored by many
But understood by few
Dark yet colorful
Complex and profound
I see the whole picture
The pieces missed by the crowd

Envelop Me

I want to bathe in the depths of your mind
Submerge me in your intellect
Shower me with your wisdom
Let me float in the sea of your desires
I promise that you will not drown me
Not even in your deepest waters
For I can tread through your fears
And endure the waves of your despair

Trojan Horse

I'm not a Trojan horse
You can let me through your walls
They're so heavily guarded
For good reason of course
But I promise you this
If you decide to let me in
You don't have to fear attack
For I am armed with only bliss

I See You

To the man who speaks through song lyrics and
quotations
Who shares his vulnerability through the guise
of others words
As if they're not emitting straight from his
beating heart
I hear you

To the man who hides his truth behind a smile
and a laugh
Who feels as though he goes by unnoticed
As if his soul doesn't shine brighter than a
beacon in the night
I see you

To the man who has been molded by his hurt and
mistreatment
Who's elusive emotions are palpable through his
bustling silence
As if I'm not fluent in the language of suffering
I understand you

To the man who has been beaten and bruised by
life's unforgiving hands

Who's bleeding heart still needs stitches from
age old battles
As if I wouldn't know how to tend to your
wounds
I'd take care of you

Kismet

I know you feel it, too
The cosmic pull
From me,
to you

www.ingramcontent.com/pod-product-compliance
Lightning Source LLC
Chambersburg PA
CBHW070730160726
48003CB00006BA/2432